SEATT

A BOOK OF 21 POST

BROWNTROUT PUBLISHERS
SAN FRANCISCO • CALIFORNIA

BROWNTROUT PUBLISHERS

P.O. BOX 280070

SAN FRANCISCO • CALIFORNIA 94128-0070

ISBN: 1-56313 826-3

TITLE #: P6826

BROWNTROUT publishes a large line of calendars, photographic books, and postcard books.

Please write for more information.

Printed in Korea

SEATTLE

Sunset afterglow on city skyline from west Seattle

BROWNTROUT PUBLISHERS • SAN FRANCISCO, CALIFORNIA

SEATTLE
Houseboats on Lake Union

PUBLISHED BY BROWNTROUT • SAN FRANCISCO, CALIFORNIA

SEATTLE
Sunset, Portage Bay from West Montlake Park

PUBLISHED BY BROWNTROUT • SAN FRANCISCO, CALIFORNIA

SEATTLE
Metropolitan Plaza

PUBLISHED BY BROWNTROUT • SAN FRANCISCO, CALIFORNIA

SEATTLE
Salmon Bay Fishermans Terminal

PUBLISHED BY BROWNTROUT • SAN FRANCISCO, CALIFORNIA

SEATTLE
City skyline from Rizal Park

PUBLISHED BY BROWNTROUT • SAN FRANCISCO, CALIFORNIA

SEATTLE

Weeping Japanese Cherry Trees and daffodils,
Washington Park Arboretum

PUBLISHED BY BROWNTROUT • SAN FRANCISCO, CALIFORNIA

SEATTLE

Overcast mist on Lake Union and The Center for Wooden Boats

PUBLISHED BY BROWNTROUT • SAN FRANCISCO, CALIFORNIA

SEATTLE
Neon coffee and market signs at dusk above the Pike Street Market

PUBLISHED BY BROWNTROUT • SAN FRANCISCO, CALIFORNIA

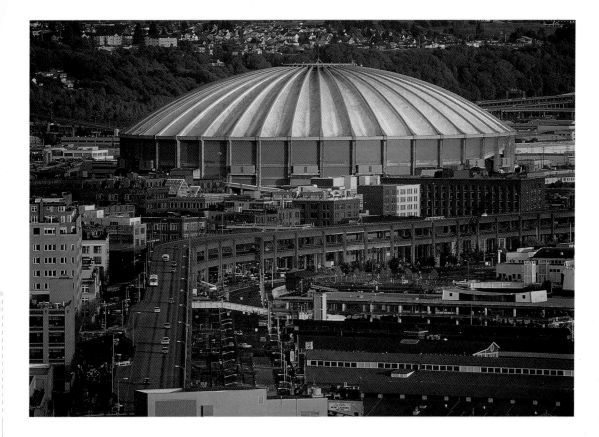

SEATTLE
The Kingdome

PUBLISHED BY BROWNTROUT • SAN FRANCISCO, CALIFORNIA

SEATTLE
City skyline from Interstate 5

PUBLISHED BY BROWNTROUT • SAN FRANCISCO, CALIFORNIA

SEATTLE

Silhouette of the BSA Statue of Liberty on Alki Beach

PUBLISHED BY BROWNTROUT • SAN FRANCISCO, CALIFORNIA

SEATTLE
Pacific First Centre

PUBLISHED BY BROWNTROUT • SAN FRANCISCO, CALIFORNIA

SEATTLE
Float plane and boats docked on Lake Union

PUBLISHED BY BROWNTROUT • SAN FRANCISCO, CALIFORNIA

SEATTLE

Blossoming cherry trees and Art Building, University of Washington

PUBLISHED BY BROWNTROUT • SAN FRANCISCO, CALIFORNIA

SEATTLE
Seattle University fountain and Christmas tree at dusk

PUBLISHED BY BROWNTROUT • SAN FRANCISCO, CALIFORNIA

SEATTLE
Cityscape

PUBLISHED BY BROWNTROUT • SAN FRANCISCO, CALIFORNIA

SEATTLE
Post Alley, Pike Street Market

PUBLISHED BY BROWNTROUT • SAN FRANCISCO, CALIFORNIA

SEATTLE
Elliott Bay, Port of Seattle and city skyline

PUBLISHED BY BROWNTROUT • SAN FRANCISCO, CALIFORNIA

SEATTLE
Japanese Maples, Washington Park Arboretum

PUBLISHED BY BROWNTROUT • SAN FRANCISCO, CALIFORNIA